Carolyn Boulton

Series consultant: Joyce Pope

Franklin Watts

London New York Toronto Sydney

First published in Great Britain in 1984
by Franklin Watts Ltd
12a Golden Square
London W1

First published in the United States of America by
Franklin Watts Inc.
387 Park Avenue South
New York
N.Y. 10016

Phototypeset by Tradespools Ltd, Frome, Somerset
Printed in Italy

UK edition:
ISBN 0 86313 131 X
US edition:
ISBN 0-531-04634-6
Library of Congress
Catalog Card Number:
84-50015

Designed by
Ben White

Illustrated by
Colin Newman, Val Sangster/
Linden Artists,
and Chris Forsey

BIRDS

Contents

Equipment

As well as a few everyday items you will need the following equipment to carry out the activities in this book.

Spiral bound notebook
Hand lens with 10× magnification on ribbon to hang around your neck
Spiral bound folder
Tweezers
Needle pushed into a cork
Plaster of Paris
Old leather gloves
Oven glove
Binoculars
Plastic bags
Mothballs (These are poisonous. Always wash your hands after using them)
Margarine and yogurt containers
Pieces of cardboard
Drawing pins
Blotting paper
Box lined with cotton
Clear plastic wrap
Old spoon and toothbrush
Paper clip
Tissue paper
Chicken egg

Introduction

Birds are animals covered with feathers. This is what sets them apart from all other creatures. Most birds can fly, but then so can bats and many insects. Feathers and flight are two things that affect the way of life of a bird.

Birds are not difficult animals to see. Most of them are busy feeding during the daytime and sleep at night. They are around you everywhere—in your playground, in the town and park, in woods and fields; along rivers or at the seaside, even out at sea or up a mountain. They are fun to watch whether feeding from breadcrumbs that you have scattered for them or flying above you as if without effort.

You will see some birds because they are large or because of their bright and colorful feathers. You might miss others because they are tiny or their feathers are the color of their surroundings. Often you know a bird is near because you can hear it singing tunefully or calling noisily. Birds live in a world of sight and sound. The other senses of taste, touch and smell that are important to you are not so necessary to them.

In this book there are activities that you can do yourself to try to discover how birds live. A feather found lying on the ground is a good beginning. It can tell you a lot about the bird that left it behind.

Feathers and flight

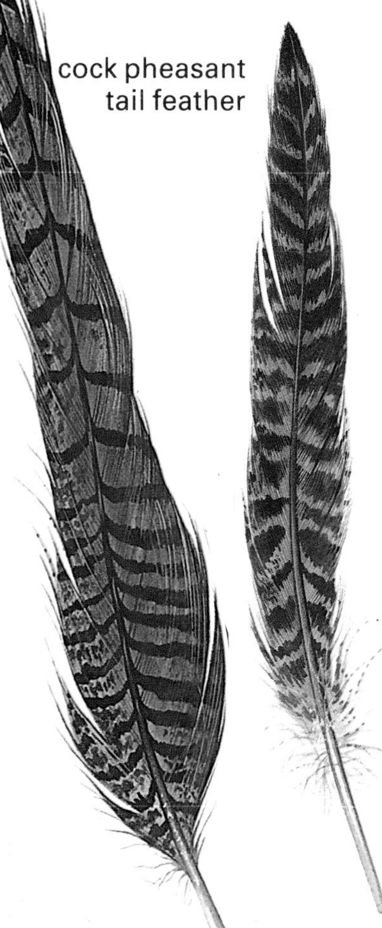

cock pheasant tail feather

hen pheasant tail feather

Feathers are the most important part of every bird. They help it to fly. A swan may have as many as 25,000 feathers over its body. A sparrow has between 2,000 and 3,000 feathers.

Feathers keep a bird warm by trapping a layer of air next to its skin. In cold weather they can be fluffed up to trap more air. They make a blanket round the bird's body. Feathers are waterproof. They keep birds dry because water runs off their oily surfaces.

Birds recognize each other by the color patterns of their feathers. These may be bright and attractive, as in a cock pheasant, for example, or they may be fairly dull as in the hen pheasant.

▷A peacock fans out the long feathers of his train. He struts and shows off his brilliant plumage to a passing peahen hoping to attract her attention. Her feathers are not so colorful. Female birds spend much time sitting still on their nests. It is important that they cannot be seen. Their inconspicuous colors help to hide them.

Looking after feathers

There are two main types of feather, down and contour. Contour feathers cover the bird's body and wings. The down feathers lie underneath, fluffy and soft, keeping the bird warm.

Contour feathers have a strong shaft and flexible vane. Look at the vane through a hand lens. It is made up of hundreds of barbs that are fringed with barbules. The barbules of one barb link together with barbules above and below it. Feathers get damaged easily and the barbules pulled apart. Birds must repair the damage so that they can fly well.

Feather-care, or preening, is an endless chore. Most birds have preen glands on their backs. A bird takes oil from this gland to rub over its feathers. This keeps the feathers waterproof. The bird gently pulls its feathers between its beak to zip up the barbules again.

◁The teal carefully preens to get rid of any dirt, fleas and mites.

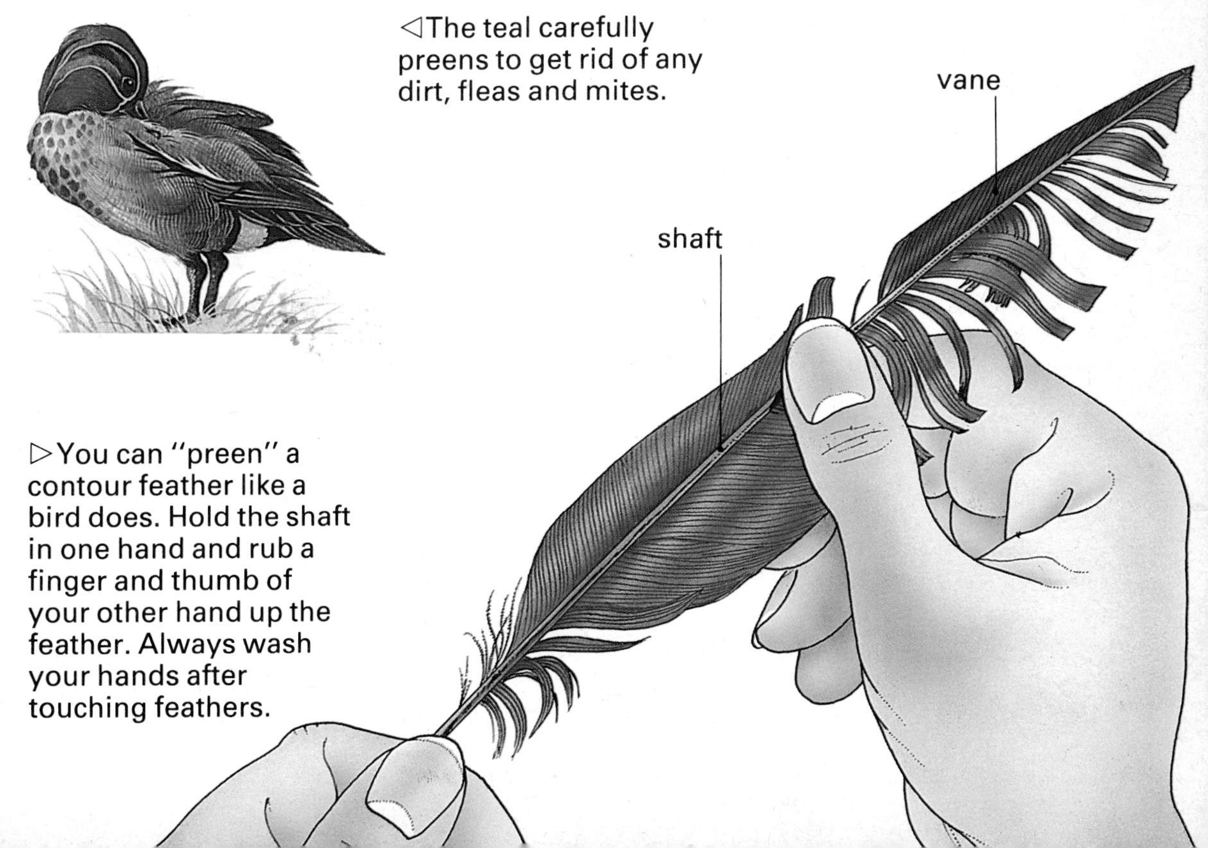

▷You can "preen" a contour feather like a bird does. Hold the shaft in one hand and rub a finger and thumb of your other hand up the feather. Always wash your hands after touching feathers.

Molting feathers

A bird's feathers take a lot of wear and tear during its life. Every year feathers are lost, or molted, and replaced with new ones. Some birds molt once a year after the breeding season. That is after the chicks have left the nest. Other birds molt twice a year, once before and then again after the breeding season.

Feathers are not living things. Old ones are pushed out of the skin by the growth of new feathers. They fall out a few at a time so that the bird is still able to fly. Usually the large wing and tail feathers are molted first, in equal numbers from each side of the bird. The body feathers are then slowly replaced over several weeks.

▽ Make a collection of feathers that you see lying on the ground, especially undamaged ones. You will find a lot in early spring and in the middle of summer. Keep them in a folder, tucking the shafts and tips under slits made in the pages. Pull the feathers downwards to stop them ruffling up. You may not know which bird the feather came from but you can say what kind it is. Most wing feathers have the shaft to one side of the vane. Tail feathers have the shaft in the middle.

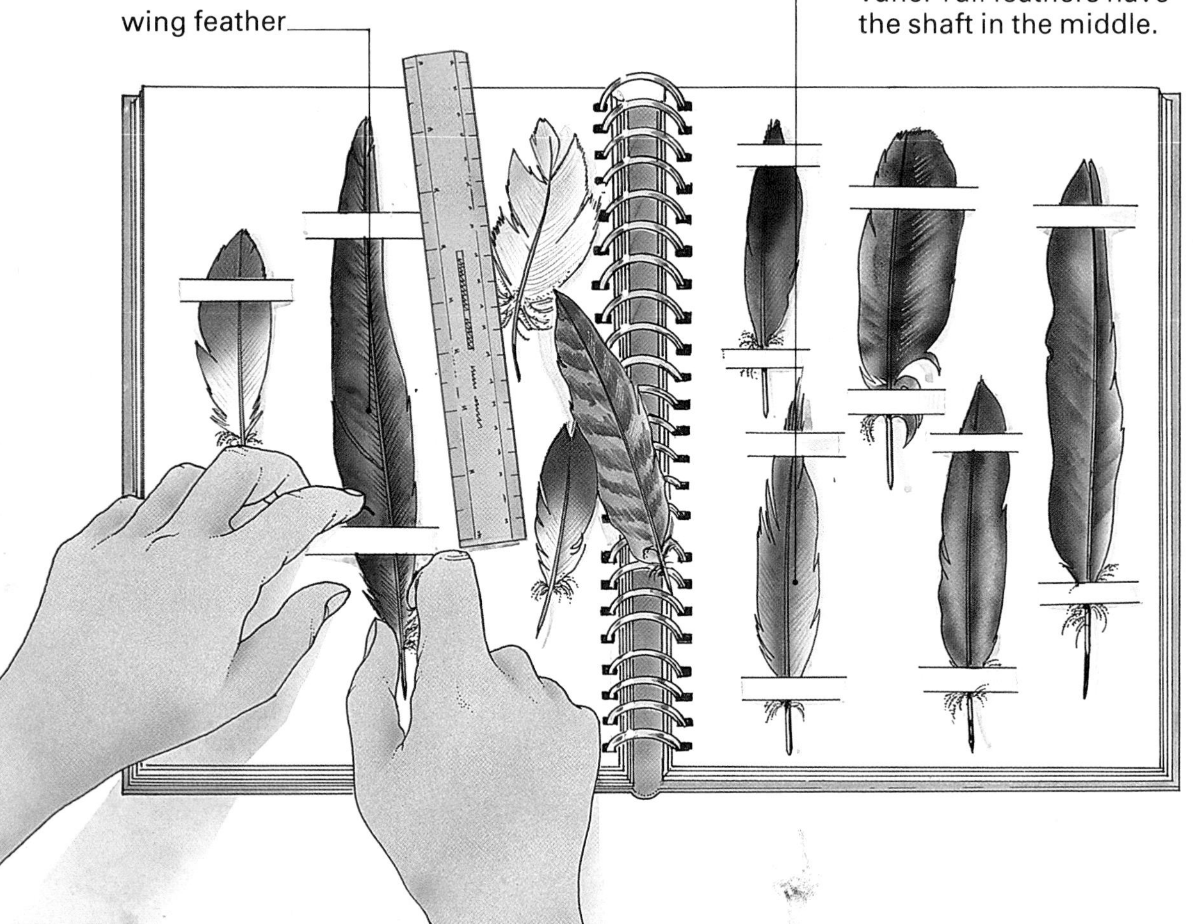

A flying machine

A bird's body is a flying machine. It is light in weight and extremely strong. The two pairs of muscles that give the bird power for flight are attached to the deep ridge along its breastbone. The larger muscles move the bird's wings downwards and backwards. The smaller muscles pull the wings up again. Other smaller muscles twist and turn the wings in flight.

The bones of the skeleton are light, but still strong. The large wing bones are hollow. They are strengthened with very thin bars that run across the inside.

Leading from the lungs is a system of air sacs, like bubbles of air, which also help to keep the bird light.

hollow wing bone

△After a chicken dinner, find one of the large wing bones. The bone is tough, so ask an adult to saw it in two pieces. You will see the very fine bars that criss-cross inside it. Be careful not to cut your fingers on the sharp edges.

How a bird flies

Lift is the force that keeps a bird in the air. As soon as the wings are moved through the air the force is produced. It works like this. The upper surface of the wing is curved. Air has farther to go over the wing than under it. The air moves faster over this curved surface making a difference in pressure above and below the wing. Because the pressure is greater below, it presses up on the underside of the wing and lifts the bird.

On the downbeat in flight, the wing feathers are tightly closed to push against the air. The bird moves forwards. On the upbeat, the primary feathers, those at the wing tip, open up to let air flow through. The secondary feathers stay closed.

▽Try this experiment to see how "lift" works. Hold one end of a strip of paper between the thumb and forefinger of each hand. Blow over the top. The paper is lifted up, not forced down. Your breath rushing over the paper reduces the pressure above it. The greater pressure below lifts the paper up.

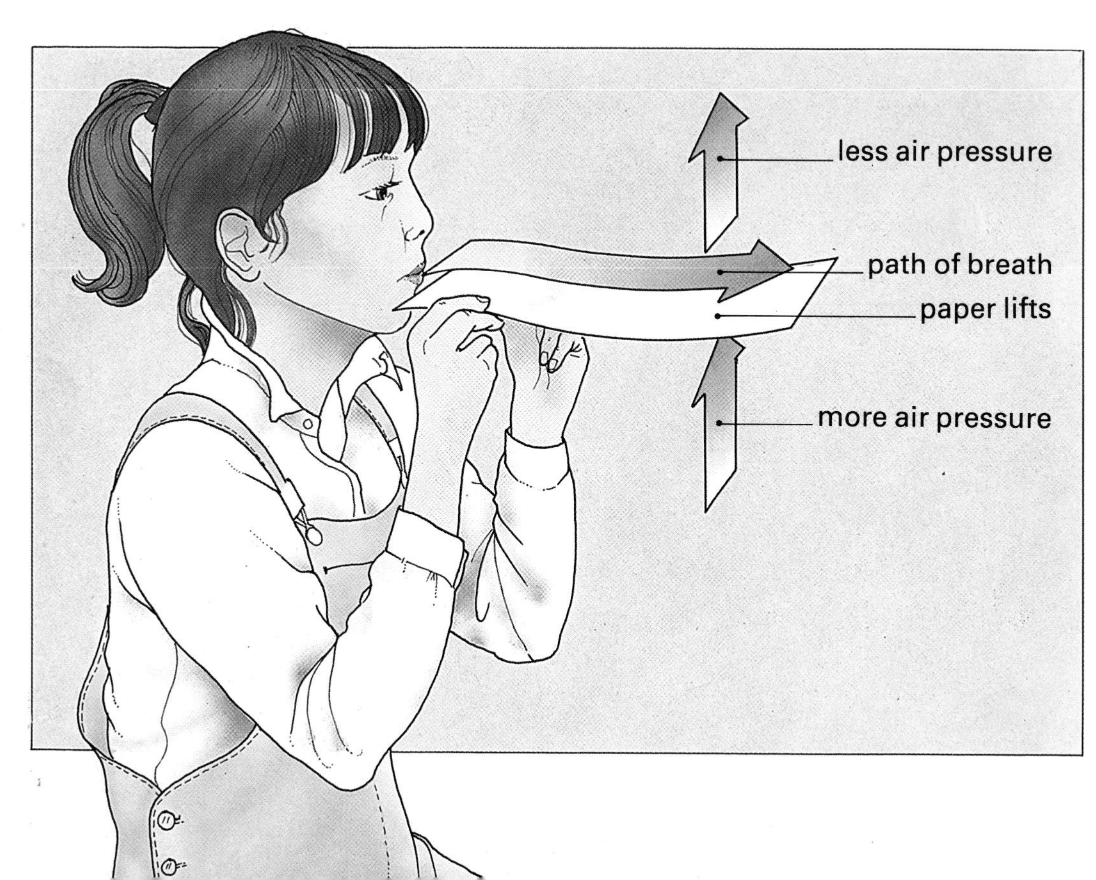

Wing shapes

The shape of the wings affects the way a bird flies. The pheasant, for example, can rise quickly from the ground by flapping its short, wide wings. They are very effective for a quick takeoff when the bird is frightened.

Fast-flying birds, such as the swallow, have thin, pointed wings. Swallows move swiftly and turn sharply in the air. Other birds, with long wings, make use of wind currents to glide and soar on. They travel great distances on their long outstretched wings. But it takes a lot of effort for the bird to keep its wings spread wide against the force of the wind.

While flying, a bird changes the angle of its wings to change direction; it beats its wings faster to increase speed. The tail is used to steer with and the alula (thumb) feathers lift to prevent the bird from stopping or stalling suddenly.

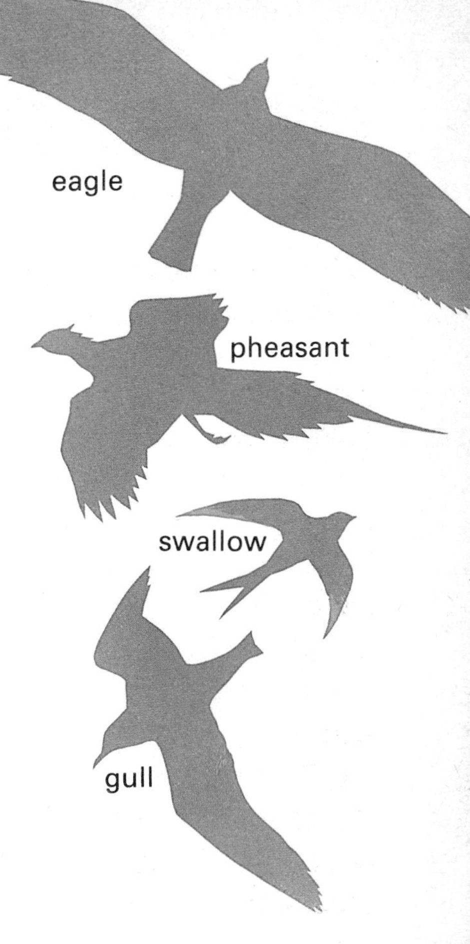

△Watch how different birds fly according to the shape of their wings. Are they flapping their wings continuously to keep airborne, or are they hardly moving their wings at all?

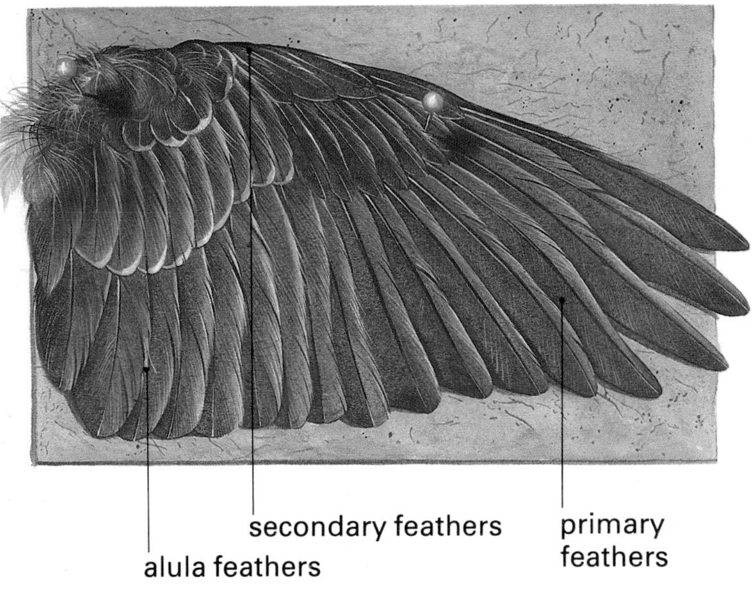

◁If you find a dead bird cut off a wing. Spread the wing out and pin it to a piece of card. Put it in a plastic bag with mothballs to kill any fleas and mites. Look at the main flight feathers. The primaries propel the bird through the air. The secondaries make up the surface for lift.

Beaks and feeding

△The oystercatcher levers open a mussel with its long sharp bill.

Birds eat all kinds of things—fruit, nuts, insects, snails, worms, other birds, fish, lizards and even eggs.

The long beak of a wading bird is used to probe deep into mud and sand for shellfish. The flat spoon-like beak of a duck sifts water for tiny animals and plants. The short, strong beak of a seed-eater is good for cracking open nuts and seeds. Owls use their strong hooked beaks to tear their food apart. The insect-eating swallow flies after insects, catching them in its very wide open mouth. Fruit-eaters have fairly long bills. Fish-eaters have sharp bills like tweezers to catch their slippery food.

Try to guess what a bird feeds on from the shape of its beak. Make a record of the favorite foods of different types of birds.

△The shoveler uses its broad bill as a sieve to dabble in the water.

△The crossbill picks the seeds out of a cone with its sharp crossed beak.

▷Look for feeding signs left by birds, for example, chipped mussel shells at the seaside, nuts pecked for the kernels, pine cones stripped of seeds and rotting apples with peck marks.

mussel

▷The barn owl tears with its beak and holds its prey with its claws.

nuts

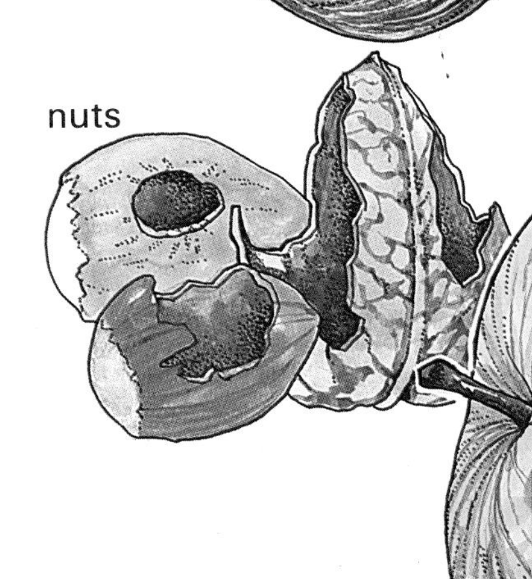

How a bird eats

A bird's beak is made of keratin, a light, hard material rather like your fingernails. The beak is used to gather food with, but as there are no teeth along it the bird cannot chew. Instead it swallows mouthfuls of food whole. The food is then broken up in the gizzard, a special muscular part of the bird's stomach.

Watch birds feeding along the sea shore or in a garden to see how they use their beaks. You can also look for feeding signs left by birds. Holes in the sand may be made by oystercatchers searching for mussels. Peck marks in an apple rotting on the ground may be the work of a starling. Birds will also pull at fir cones to get at the seeds and chip away at nutshells.

Remember that other animals, such as squirrels and mice, also enjoy these foods. Try to learn the difference between "teeth" marks and "beak" marks.

△The starling eats many kinds of food. It has a stabbing beak.

△The insect-eating swallow catches food while on the wing.

△The waxwing has a pointed beak. It is a berry-eater.

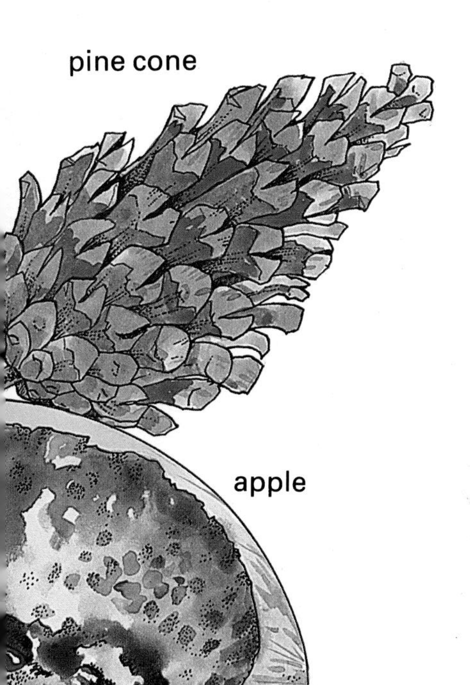

◁The heron catches fish between the two parts of its long bill.

Pellets

Pellets are hard lumps of food that a bird has not been able to digest. Instead of getting rid of this undigested food as a dropping the bird coughs it up out of its beak. It is not the same as vomiting but it is a natural thing for many birds to do.

Pellets are made in the gizzard. Their size and shape depend on the size of the bird's throat. Large birds can cough up large pellets. Fresh pellets are covered with slimy mucus that eases them along the throat. This mucus hardens into a crust once the pellet is out.

barn owl pellet

△The barn owl's pellets are smooth, firm and clean to handle. They are rounded with a diameter of about 1½ in (38 mm). You may find them where the owl roosts.

△The herring gull eats almost anything, from fish to silver paper, and makes messy pellets about 2 in (52 mm) long. You may find these pellets under its nest site.

herring gull pellet

Taking a pellet apart

Many birds make pellets. You may find pellets by searching the ground under large trees in woods or a park where you know these birds nest or roost. Do this in autumn and winter, not in the breeding season, when you might disturb nesting birds.

Once you know of a barn owl's roost, for example, you will be able to collect its pellets regularly. It usually makes two a day. By taking the pellets apart carefully you will get a good idea of what the owl has been feeding on. There may be bones of birds and mammals and the wing cases of beetles all wrapped up in fur or feathers.

To take a pellet apart, you need a dish of warm water, a needle pushed into a cork, tweezers, blotting paper and a hand lens. Break the pellet in half and soak the halves in the water for a couple of hours. The feathers and fur will float free. Pour off the dirty water and separate the bones with the needle. Pick them out with the tweezers and dry them on the blotting paper.

▽Draw, weigh and measure the pellet. Make a note of where you found it. After dissecting it look at the tiny bones with a hand lens. Count the bones. There may be a hundred or more. It is not always possible to say which animals the bones came from—barn owls eat mice, voles and shrews among other things. Display the bones on a piece of paper or keep them in labeled matchboxes.

Feet and legs

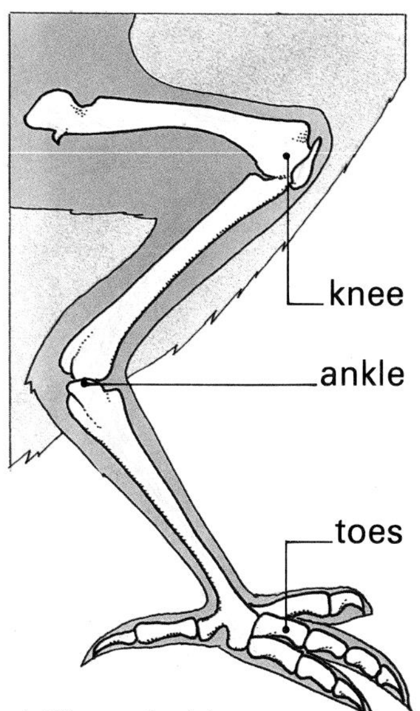

△The perching wren stands on its toes. Its ankles are off the ground, its knees high up. The legs help to absorb the shock when a bird lands after flight.

Most birds are able to walk on land as well as fly through the air. Some birds perch and hop from branch to branch, while others walk or run, swim, wade or climb up trees. They use their feet to grip their food, scratch their heads and preen their feathers.

A bird has four toes on which it stands. Usually, three point forward and one back. A waterside bird, such as the heron, has long legs and toes that are spread wide apart. It can walk in water on soft mud without sinking. Swimming birds, like ducks, have webbed feet and legs near the back of their bodies. This makes walking on land awkward but the feet are very good for swimming. Birds of prey, such as eagles, have feet that do a special job. The strong, fierce talons grip and kill the birds' food.

△Most woodpeckers have strong claws and two toes pointing backward, and two forward. This helps the bird grip the tree as it climbs.

△The peregrine falcon has large deadly talons, or claws, with which it kills. The falcon will "swoop" through the sky to strike at a flying bird.

△The mallard has webbed feet. The webs make a large surface that pushes against the water and propels the bird forward.

▽Gallinule footprints in wet mud are ideal for making a cast. (Instructions are given below.) It is best to let the plaster dry for a couple of hours before taking the circle of cardboard away from it. Put the cast in a sunny place for a week to dry out completely. Then brush off any mud with an old toothbrush. You can paint the footprint with a water-base paint and varnish it if you wish.

Making a plaster cast

Try making a plaster cast of a bird's footprint. You need Plaster of Paris, water, a large yogurt container, an old spoon, a piece of cardboard bent into a circle and held with a paper clip and some tissue paper.

Half fill the pot with water and add the plaster, stirring all the time until you have a thick paste that will pour. Put the cardboard around the footprint and push it a short way into the ground. Pour the mixture over the print and leave it to set for ten minutes. When it is hard, take the cast from the ground and wrap it in tissue paper to take home.

Nests and nesting

△Golden eagles always return to the same eyrie, or nest, adding more sticks each season.

△The male starling makes an untidy nest of grass and straw in a hole in a tree.

▷Both cock and hen magpies make their large cup-like nests in the tops of trees. The nest is built of prickly sticks lined with mud. Above the nest is a roof of sticks. The entrance is on the cup-edge.

A bird builds a nest as a home in which to lay and hatch eggs and look after the young chicks. In spring, before the start of the nesting season, the male bird, the cock, claims a piece of land to be his own. This is his own home ground, or territory. He keeps other similar birds away from his territory so that they do not compete with him for food.

The golden eagle, for example, has a very large territory, often 3 miles (5 km) across. He spends a long time hunting for his food and needs this vast area to find enough grouse, ptarmigans, snakes and other small animals to feed on. Other birds, such as cliff-nesting kittiwakes, live in a large group or colony. There is plenty of food in the sea and so it does not matter that they live close together.

The cock has to attract a hen and court her. She usually chooses the site for the nest. They may build it together or one bird may make the nest on its own.

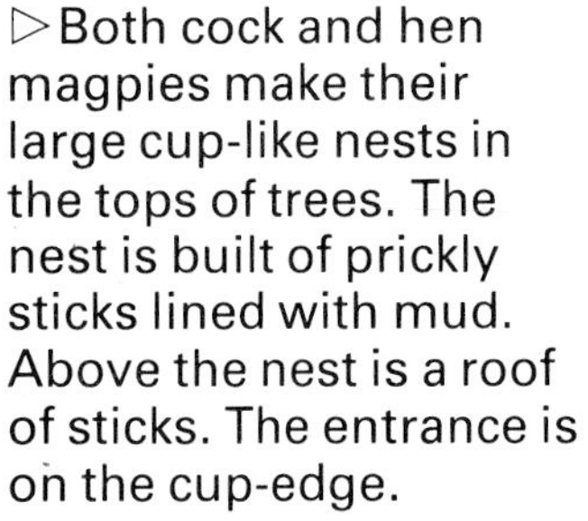

Where to build?

Nests are built in all shapes, sizes and places, depending on the kind of bird. The materials used include mud, sticks, grass, straw, seaweed, leaves, pieces of bark, flower heads, wool, hair, feathers, cobwebs and moss for a soft lining.

Wherever a bird decides to build its home, it must be in a place safe from enemies. There must also be plenty of food around. Birds that spend a lot of their time perching in trees naturally build their nests on tree branches or in tree holes. Birds that live by the sea, getting their food from the water, nest along cliffs or sand dunes.

Most birds return to the same area to breed year after year, but not necessarily to the same nest or with the same partner.

△Gallinules build their "raft" nests, piling up the material so that the eggs are above the water.

△Swallows make their nests on ledges of buildings or branches.

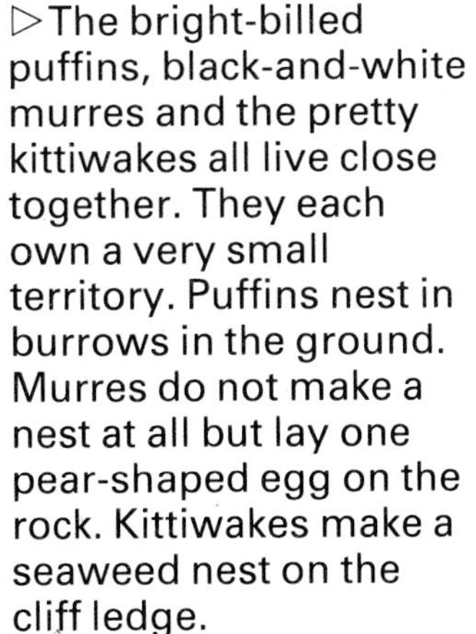

▷The bright-billed puffins, black-and-white murres and the pretty kittiwakes all live close together. They each own a very small territory. Puffins nest in burrows in the ground. Murres do not make a nest at all but lay one pear-shaped egg on the rock. Kittiwakes make a seaweed nest on the cliff ledge.

Nesting materials

Birds use a great number of different materials for nest building. In early spring you can collect together bundles of things to hang up on a tree or wall and watch the birds that take bits and pieces from them. The bundles can be made up of dog, cat or human hair combings, cotton, wool, strips of paper, strips of silver foil, grass, straw, small twigs, leaves, moss and flowers.

Watch the birds that come to the bundles and keep a record of what you see. To do this, make a chart listing the materials on the left hand side of a piece of paper and the birds that fly to them along the top. Put a tick against the bird's name and against the material that it takes. In this way you will get some idea of what birds use in nest building.

bundle of materials

◁Stand in a place where you can see the birds but they cannot see you. Note the date that you make your observations. Watch over a period of several days, perhaps at different times. It may take a little time for the birds to notice the bundles so you will need to be patient.

Inside a nest

Some birds may make their nests in a few hours; others may take days. However long it takes, a bird has to work very hard. It has to fly back and forth countless times to its nest site, carrying twigs and other things a little at a time. The bird does all this work with its beak. It collects the materials and weaves them into a strong, safe home in which to bring up its young.

When trees are leafless, in late autumn, you may see a nest on a branch. Look at the nest over several days to make sure it is no longer being used before taking it home to study more closely. Never disturb nests in the breeding season during spring and summer.

▽If you find an abandoned nest take it carefully from the tree. Protect your hands with old leather gloves. Put the nest in a plastic bag with some mothballs for a few days so that the insects crawl out and die. Draw the nest, weigh and measure it and note where you found it. Now gently take it apart with tweezers. The bird started building from the outside, so you must start from the inside. How many different materials were used to make the nest?

Eggs

All female birds lay eggs. After mating, the hen lays a group, or clutch, of several eggs. Together, the parents keep the eggs warm and safe in the nest. During this period, called incubation, each egg grows into a chick. When it is ready the chick hatches out of the shell. It uses a little spike, or "egg tooth," on its upper beak to cut through the shell. The egg tooth disappears later.

After hatching, the chicks are cared for by the parents until they are able to look after themselves. Some chicks, ducklings, for example, are able to walk and find food right away. Other chicks, such as baby wrens, are helpless for a couple of weeks.

▽Crack open a chicken's egg to see the different parts inside. Feel how strong the shell is. Sometimes you will see a tiny red spot on the yellow yolk. This is the germ cell which develops into a chick in the egg of a wild bird. The yolk is food for the growing chick. The white albumen is a protective cushion, which contains liquid and some vital foods for the young chick.

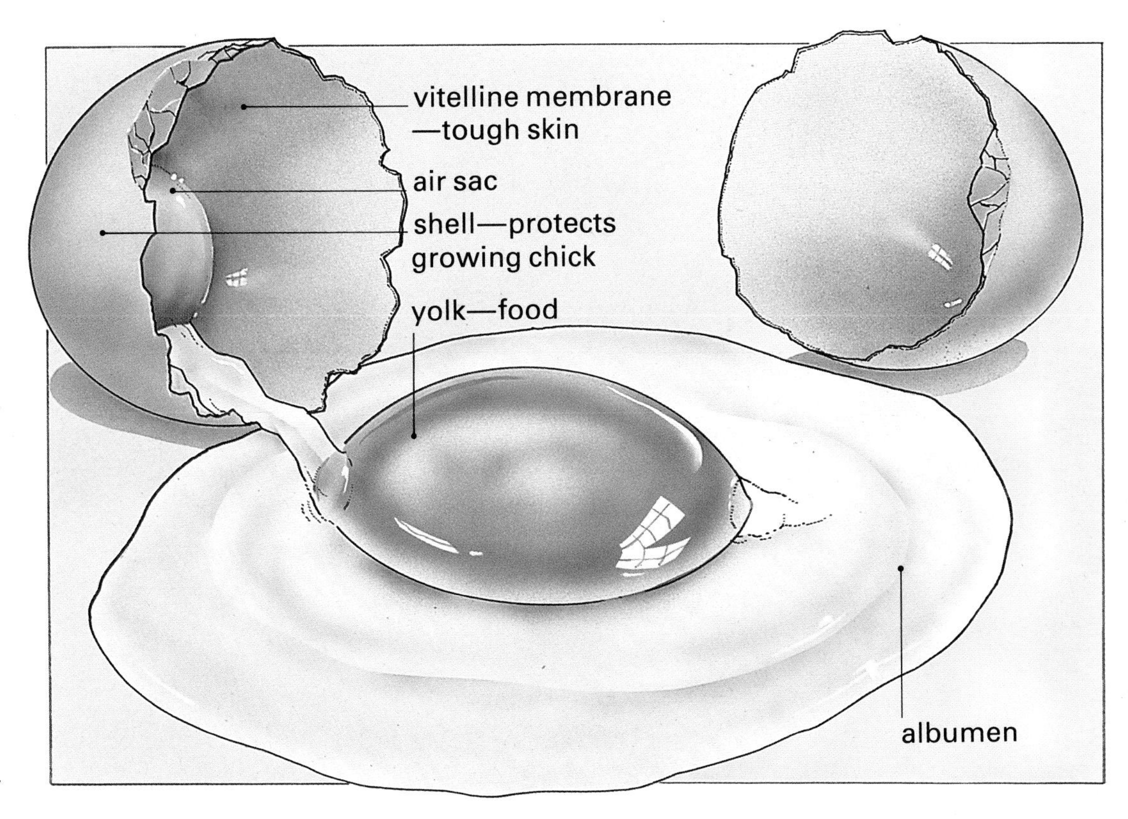

▷Make a collection of broken shells. Never take eggs from nests. Parent birds drop old shells over the side of the nest or carry them away. If they did not, the white inside of the shell might attract a predator to the nest. Keep the pieces in a box lined with cotton and covered with clear plastic wrap. You can remove this to add more shells.

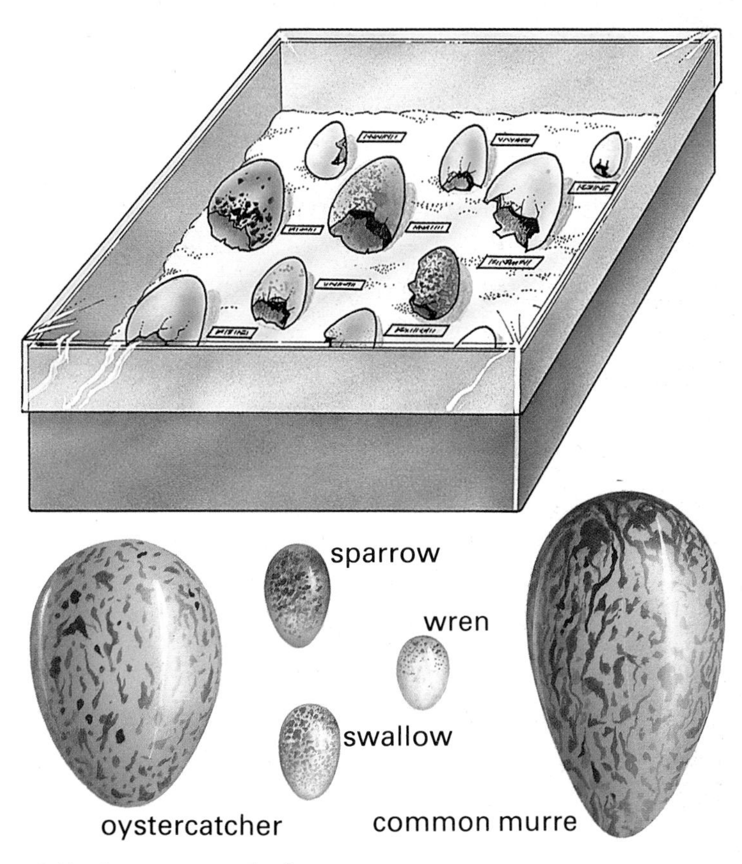

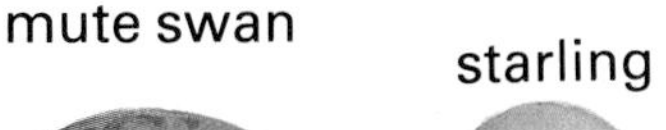

All shapes and sizes

The tiny wren lays two clutches a year, each of 5 or 6 eggs. The large mute swan lays one clutch of 5–8 eggs. They are about seven times larger than the wren's eggs and take more than twice as long to hatch.

Most eggs are blunt at one end and pointed at the other. Look at the pear-shaped egg of the murre. This bird lays only one egg straight on the cliff ledge. It does not make a nest. If the egg is knocked, it rolls around in a circle, not off the cliff edge.

Eggshells are often colored and speckled so that they do not show up in the nest. Blue eggs are usually laid by birds that nest in a shaded place, such as a hedge. White eggs are laid by birds that nest in holes. It does not matter that the eggs are conspicuous there.

Feeding birds

In winter, small birds can lose up to one third of their body weight each night just trying to keep warm. By putting out food in the morning in your garden or playground you could be saving their lives.

Collect foods from the countryside in the autumn. Ripe berries can be stored in a dry, dark place until needed. Pick up beechnuts, acorns, horse and sweet chestnuts from the ground soon after they have fallen.

Kitchen scraps of bread crumbs, stale cake and bruised fruit can be put out. Do not give birds salted peanuts or shredded coconut. And do not give them too much white bread as this swells up in their stomachs.

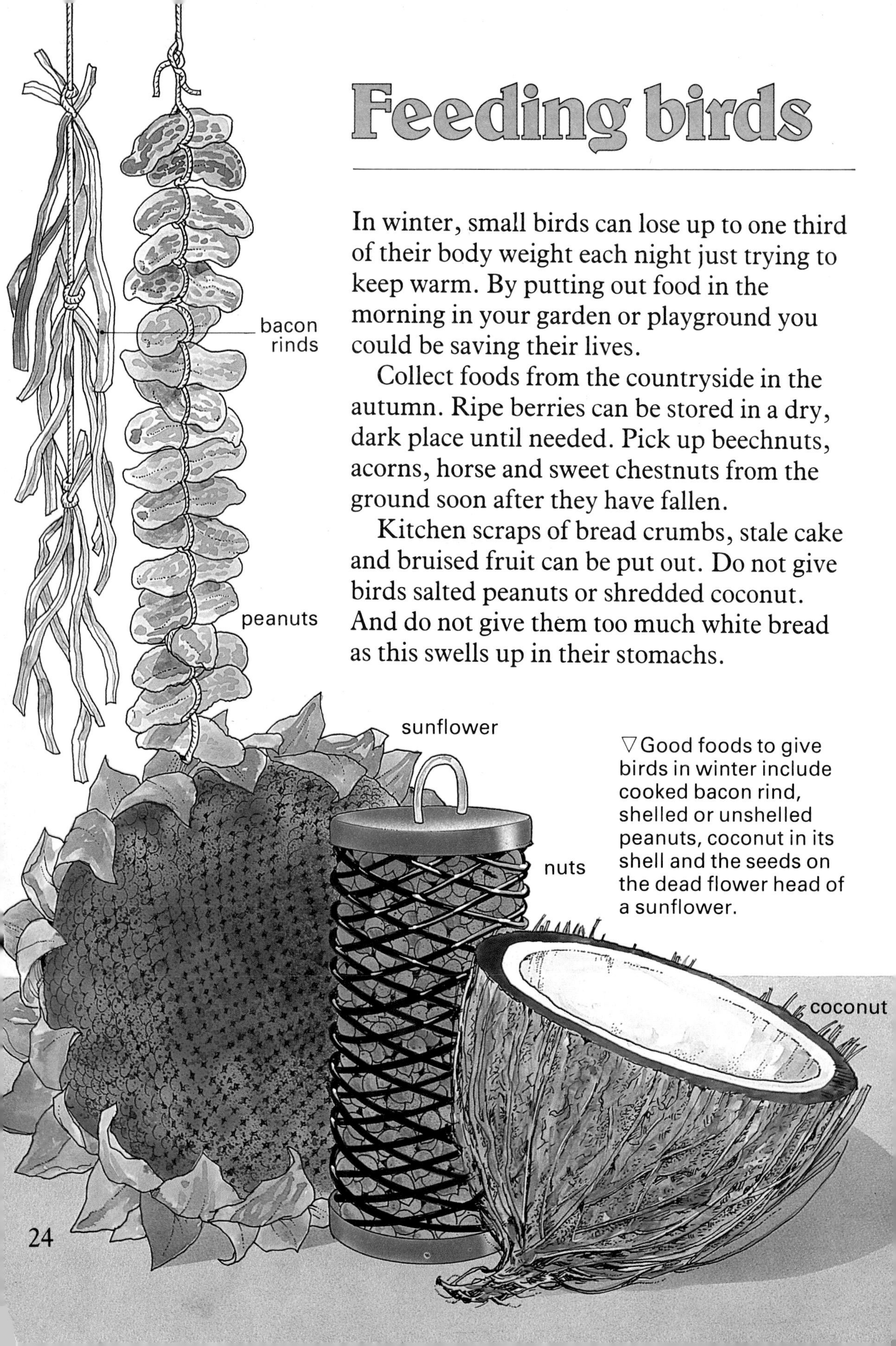

▽ Good foods to give birds in winter include cooked bacon rind, shelled or unshelled peanuts, coconut in its shell and the seeds on the dead flower head of a sunflower.

Bird pudding

You can make a special bird pudding to feed birds. Thread some string through the base of an old margarine container or coconut shell and secure the string with a large knot. Put a mixture of chopped peanuts, cake and other food scraps into the pot. Melt some lard or other fat and pour this over the scraps. You will need ½ lb (¼ kg) of fat for each 1 lb (½ kg) of scraps. Leave the pudding to set before hanging it outside.

Unshelled peanuts strung on a piece of thin wire or string will attract birds such as the chickadees. The birds seem to enjoy swinging around as they eat. Shelled peanuts can be hung in a wire basket. Do not use a basket that is made with a flexible spiral wire. As one bird flies away, the wire could spring back and trap the feet of another bird feeding on the nuts.

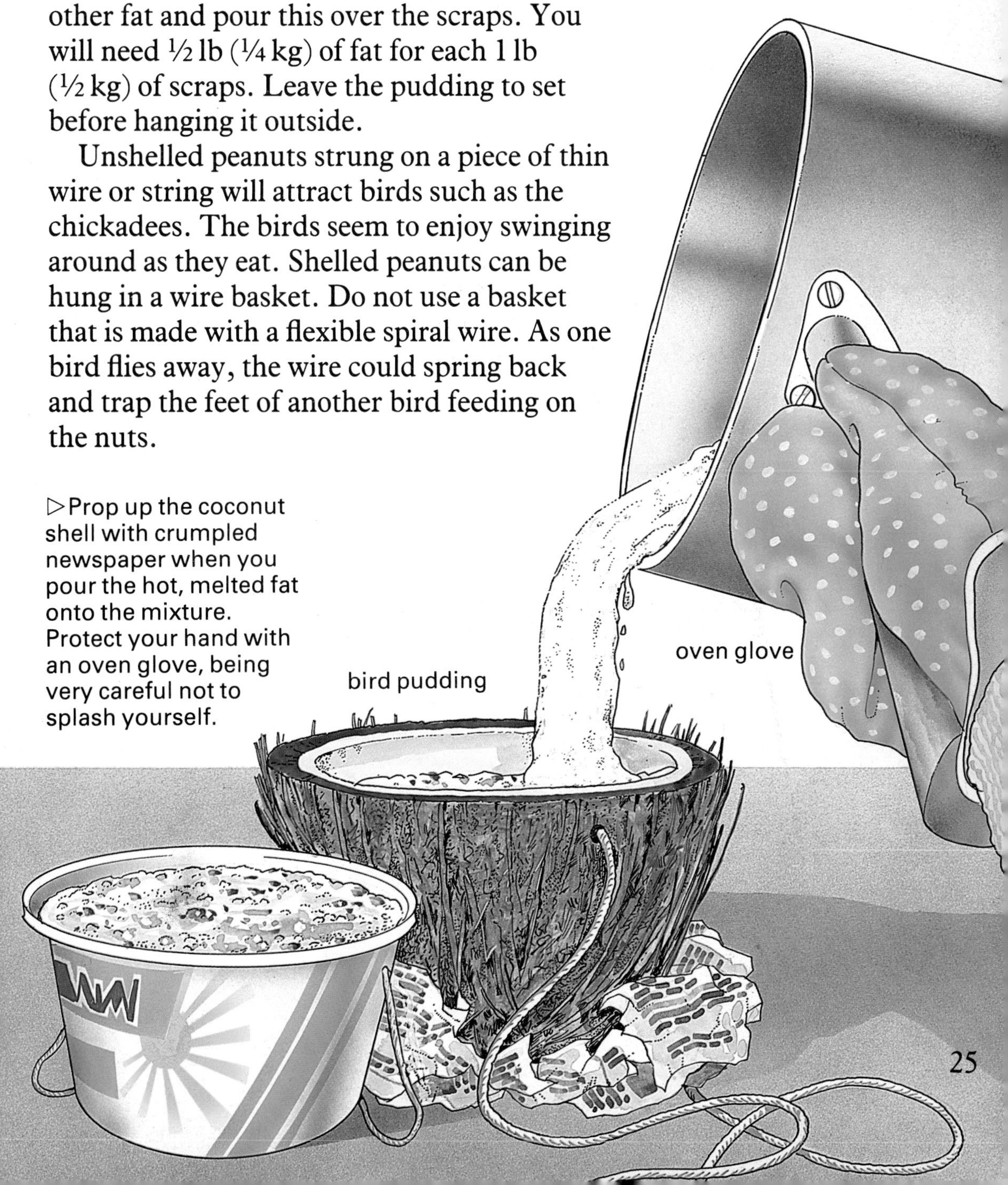

▷Prop up the coconut shell with crumpled newspaper when you pour the hot, melted fat onto the mixture. Protect your hand with an oven glove, being very careful not to splash yourself.

Birds in the garden

A bird table with plenty of food on will attract many kinds of birds. It should be about 20 in × 10 in (50 cm × 25 cm). Narrow strips of edging around the platform stop food falling off. Leave spaces at the corners to allow you to clean the table regularly. The supporting pole should be about 3 ft (1 m) high, smooth and bark-free so that cats cannot climb up it. An old tin put upside down under the table will stop cats and squirrels and other animals from climbing up the pole.

Put the table in a place where you can see the birds feeding. Ideally, it should be near shrub cover for shy birds, but not too close to branches where cats can hide. Watch the birds from a window. Do they eat at the table or take the food away? Do they have favorite foods?

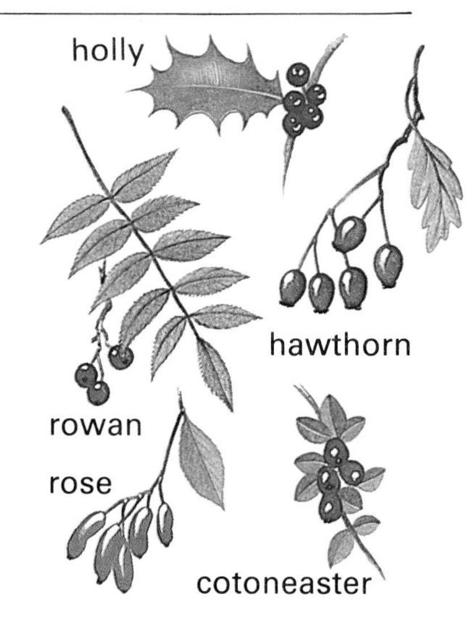

△Fruit-eating birds enjoy winter berries. By growing shrubs with berries in your garden or school grounds you will provide a natural source of food that attracts many birds.

▷Starlings peck greedily at rotting apples. They are noisy and quarrelsome and bully other birds away from food. To avoid this, put scraps out first thing in the morning before the starlings leave their roosts and in the late afternoon when they have flown back.

Once you start feeding birds in winter it is very important to put food out every day. They start to rely on you when their natural foods become frozen into the ground. You can help them by digging over a little patch of soil so that it is loose enough for them to get at worms and insects. If you scatter food on the ground, put enough just for the day. Make sure that none is left overnight as this encourages rats and mice.

An upturned trash can lid supported on bricks makes a good shallow bird bath. It also provides a drinking place for birds all year round.

Birdwatching

▽Never be without a notebook and pencil when you are birdwatching. It is important to make notes about the birds at the time you see them rather than later. If you don't, you quickly forget little details. Wear strong shoes or boots and dull-colored clothes that do not rustle when you move about.

Birdwatching is an inexpensive hobby and the more experienced you get, the more interesting it becomes. At first it is a good idea to go out with an experienced birdwatcher. Slowly you will find that you can recognize birds by their song, colors, size and flight.

All you need is a notebook, preferably spiral bound with a hard back, and pencils. Record the date, weather and place that you are visiting. Make notes and sketches, as detailed as possible, of the birds that you see so that you can look them up later in a guide book.

Binoculars are useful but not essential (7×50 is a good magnification). They should be as light as possible so that you can wear them around your neck all the time.

Before setting off on a birdwatching expedition think about what you might need. Are you going to the town park, to the seaside, to a lake or a wood? Plastic bags are useful for putting feathers in, and empty matchboxes can be used for broken eggshells. You may see footprints in sand or mud, in which case the plaster cast kit would be useful. The clothes you wear are important too. They should be warm and waterproof but not brightly colored. Shorts are not a good idea. They give little protection against sharp branches and bushes.

Try to walk quietly and carefully and do not make sudden movements.

△A good place to see birds is near a town lake or pond where birds are used to people. If you are watching in the countryside, hide among the plants and shrubs. Make yourself as comfortable as possible so that you can spend several hours looking at the many kinds of waterbirds. You will see them swim, feed, preen, react to each other, take off in flight and come in to land.

Glossary

Breeding season
Spring is the time of year when birds lay their eggs and bring up their young. Hen and cock birds form a pair. They build a nest in which the eggs are laid and incubated. Once they hatch, the chicks are looked after by the parents until they are ready to leave the nest, in the summer.

Gizzard
This is part of a bird's stomach, in the middle of its body. The bird cannot chew with its beak. It swallows its food whole. The muscular gizzard breaks up the food. Some birds swallow small pebbles, gravel, shells or fruit stones to help in the grinding process.

Incubation
The eggs laid in a nest by a hen bird must be kept at a temperature that is near to the body heat of the parent if they are to grow into chicks. To do this the bird sits on, or incubates, the eggs. Usually hen and cock birds share this task although the hen does most of the work.

Ornithology
This is the study of birds. An ornithologist is a person who studies birds.

Parts of a bird
Before you can make descriptive notes about a bird that you see you need to know the names of the various parts of its body. Try to learn the names on the drawing below. You will find them useful when using bird guide books.

Parts of a bird

Preening
This is the care a bird takes of its feathers. It "zips" up damaged feathers with its beak and takes oil from the oil gland on its back to smear over its feathers to keep them waterproof. It scratches its head feathers with its foot. All this is important for keeping the feathers in perfect condition for flight.

Roost
This is the place where a bird sleeps. A bird may sleep alone or in the company of many others. The roost must be a sheltered place where the birds can keep warm and be safe from predators. Some birds sleep in a crack or hole in a tree or building. Other birds fly far across the country to their tree roosts. Starlings, for example, follow the same flight-paths each dusk. They gather together in thousands at night.

Territory
A piece of ground that a cock bird guards against birds of the same kind. Territories are taken in the breeding season. Nesting birds find their food in this chosen area so they must keep away other birds that would eat the same food.

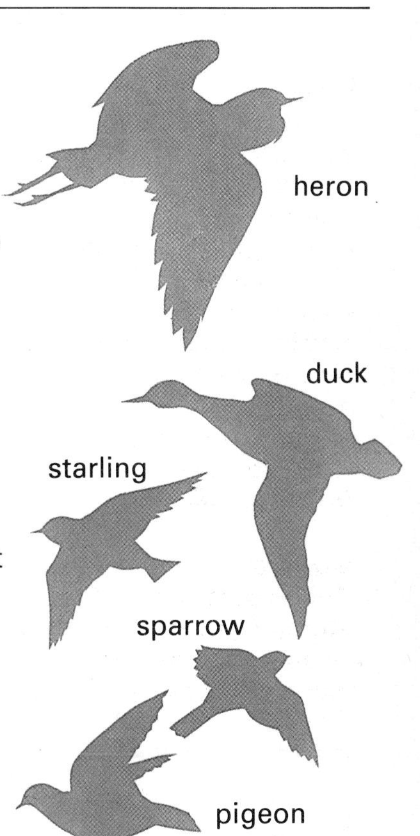

△Some birds are easy to recognize even if you only see them silhouetted against the sky. The heron flys with its legs trailing, head tucked in. Ducks fly with their necks stretched out.

Geese

Starlings

◁Birds can be recognized by their different flight patterns. Geese fly together in a 'V' shape. Starlings fly in great flocks. They twist and turn all together across the sky as they travel to and from their roosts.

Index